EGYPTIAN MYTHOLOGY

ANUBIS

BY ALLAN MOREY

CONTENT CONSULTANT
KASIA SZPAKOWSKA, PhD
PROFESSOR EMERITUS OF EGYPTOLOGY

Kids Core
An Imprint of Abdo Publishing
abdobooks.com

abdobooks.com

Printed in the United States of America, North Mankato, Minnesota.
052022
092022

 THIS BOOK CONTAINS RECYCLED MATERIALS

Cover Photos: Shutterstock Images, background; Olga Chernyak/Shutterstock Images, Anubis
Interior Photos: DEA/G. Dagli Orti/De Agostini/Getty Images, 4–5, 28 (top); Olga Chernyak/Shutterstock Images, 7, 16; Lanmas/Alamy, 9, 29 (bottom); Vladimir Zadvinskii/Shutterstock Images, 10, 29 (top); Leemage/Corbis Historical Collection/Getty Images, 12–13; Ivy Close Images/Alamy, 14, 28 (bottom); Jakub Kyncl/Shutterstock Images, 18–19; Robert Harding Productions/Alamy, 21; Charles Walker Collection/Alamy, 22; Shutterstock Images, 24, 25; Bas Photo/Shutterstock Images, 26

Editor: Layna Darling
Series Designer: Ryan Gale

Library of Congress Control Number: 2021952323

Publisher's Cataloging-in-Publication Data

Names: Morey, Allan, author.
Title: Anubis / by Allan Morey
Description: Minneapolis, Minnesota : Abdo Publishing, 2023 | Series: Egyptian mythology | Includes online resources and index.
Identifiers: ISBN 9781532198656 (lib. bdg.) | ISBN 9781644947739 (pbk.) | ISBN 9781098272302 (ebook)
Subjects: LCSH: Anubis (Egyptian deity)--Juvenile literature. | Egypt--Religion--Juvenile literature. | Gods, Egyptian--Juvenile literature. | Mythology, Egyptian--Juvenile literature.
Classification: DDC 932.01--dc23

CONTENTS

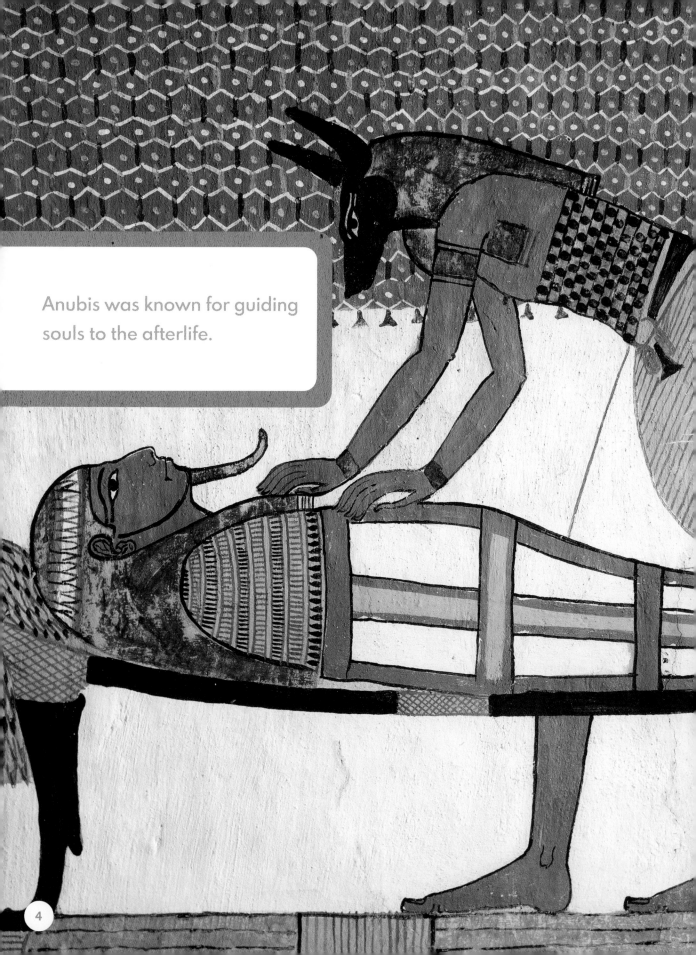

Anubis was known for guiding souls to the afterlife.

CHAPTER 1

GUIDE TO THE AFTERLIFE

In an ancient Egyptian temple, a dead body rested on a stone slab. Priests readied the body for burial. The god Anubis would arrive when they finished. He would guide the dead person's spirit to the afterlife.

The priests mummified the body. They said prayers while they worked. They dried out the body with special salts. They wrapped it in strips of linen. They also put a mask over the dead person's face.

The priests placed the body in a coffin. They moved the coffin into a tomb. Then Anubis appeared. He woke the dead person's spirit.

Tombs

Some bodies were laid to rest in ancient Egyptian tombs. The tombs might contain jars of food. The dead people's clothing and jewelry were sometimes placed there too. Some tombs even had weapons and furniture. Ancient Egyptians believed the dead might need these items in the afterlife.

Canopic Jars

 Hapi had a baboon head and watched over the person's lungs.

 Duamutef had a jackal head and looked after the person's stomach.

 Qebehsenuef had a falcon head and took care of the person's intestines.

 Imsety had a human head and guarded the person's liver.

When preparing the body for burial, priests placed a dead person's organs in special funeral jars. These jars were called canopic jars. The lids of these jars were often shaped as the four sons of Horus. The sons were Hapi, Duamutef, Qebehsenuef, and Imsety.

Anubis led the spirit to the Hall of Judgement. There, Osiris, the god of the dead, judged the spirit.

Maat, the goddess of truth, was in the Hall. She pulled a white feather from her headdress. Maat placed the feather on one side of a large golden scale. The dead person's heart was placed on the other side. This was called the Weighing of the Heart ceremony.

If the heart was lighter than the feather, the person had done good acts in life. Anubis would take the spirit to the Field of Reeds. Osiris ruled this paradise. The spirit would live there forever. If the heart was heavier, that meant the person did evil acts in life. The goddess Ammit would eat the heart. The person's spirit would no longer exist.

After a favorable judgement, Anubis would lead
the spirit to the afterlife.

Anubis played an important role in how ancient Egyptians treated their dead.

Egyptian Mythology

Ancient Egypt was a civilization that began about 5,000 years ago. People in ancient Egypt used myths to understand the world. Myths were part of the ancient Egyptians' religion. These stories explained how the world came to be. They also told ancient Egyptians how to treat their dead.

Anubis is one of many gods in Egyptian mythology. He protected souls after they died. Anubis watched over the **embalming** process. He also guarded graves. But his most important role was guiding the spirits of the dead to the afterlife.

Explore Online

Visit the website below. Does it give any new information about Anubis?

The Journey of the Dead

abdocorelibrary.com/anubis

Anubis, *left*, was a protector of souls. He protected his father, Osiris, *right*.

CHAPTER 2

PROTECTOR OF SOULS

Anubis was the son of the god Osiris and the goddess Nephthys. Anubis served his father by guiding the spirits of the dead to the afterlife. Anubis also played a key role in protecting his father after Osiris died.

Anubis helped preserve Osiris's body.

Death of Osiris

Seth was Osiris's brother. He was jealous of Osiris's power. Seth took out his anger by killing his brother. Then he spread different pieces of Osiris's body around Egypt.

The goddess Isis was Osiris's wife. She searched for her husband's body. Anubis joined Isis in the search. After all the pieces were found, Anubis embalmed Osiris's body. He preserved it from decaying. This was the first time anyone had done this. With Isis's help, Anubis performed the burial **rites** for his father. He also watched over his father's body until Osiris was brought back to life.

Osiris could no longer stay in the world of the living. He became the god of the dead. Anubis then became the guide of the dead. That is how he came to oversee the embalming process.

Changing Stories

Myths can change over time. Early myths once said that Anubis was the god of the dead. His father was Ra, the sun god. Osiris was the god of **fertility**. But as worship of Osiris grew, so did his importance. The myths changed to feature Osiris more. In these, he was god of the dead, and Anubis was his son.

One of the most important myths involving Anubis was the Weighing of the Heart ceremony.

Guiding the Dead

Anubis was not part of as many myths as some of the other gods and goddesses. That is because Anubis spent his time guiding the dead from one life to the next. He protected the dead. This was a very important role.

Anubis helped with ancient Egyptians' journeys to the afterlife in many ways. He created a way to preserve their bodies through mummification. He made sure they received their burial rites. These included prayers and spells. Anubis also guided them to the Weighing of the Heart ceremony.

Further Evidence

Look at the website below. Does it give any new information to support Chapter Two?

Anubis

abdocorelibrary.com/anubis

Ancient Egyptians painted Anubis on tombs to protect graves.

CHAPTER 3

ANUBIS IN ANCIENT EGYPT

Ancient Egyptians believed their bodies needed to be preserved to reach the afterlife. For them, honoring Anubis was necessary. He oversaw the processes that prepared their bodies for the journey.

Ancient Egyptians built **shrines** to Anubis throughout much of ancient Egypt. Most of the shrines were in the temples of other gods. But the center for his worship was in Cynopolis. This city was in northern ancient Egypt.

Ancient Egyptians asked for Anubis's protection through decorations in their tombs. They were buried with items they would need in the afterlife. These items included clay bowls and expensive jewelry.

Some ancient Egyptians believed Anubis would keep these valuables safe from grave robbers. They put statues or drawings of him around the tomb to protect their belongings. They believed the god would punish anyone who disturbed their tombs.

This statue of Anubis was found in the pharaoh Tutankhamun's tomb.

The Opening of the Mouth ceremony was an important funeral ritual.

Opening of the Mouth Ceremony

Ancient Egyptians did not see death as the end. It was an important stage in their lives. It was a way for them to honor the gods. It was also a time for their actions to be judged.

One of the most important rituals was the opening of the mouth ceremony. It happened before a person's mummified body was placed in a tomb. One priest wore an Anubis mask.

It had the head of a jackal. He held the person's coffin upright. Another priest used special instruments to touch the mummy's mouth. Ancient Egyptians believed this ritual allowed the dead person to see, speak, and eat. They believed the dead would need to do these things on their journey with Anubis to the afterlife.

Book of the Dead

The *Book of the Dead* is more than 4,000 years old. It is a collection of spells and rituals. These told ancient Egyptians how to prepare people for burial. Ancient Egyptians believed the rituals readied the dead for the journey to the afterlife. The *Book of the Dead* also described what to expect in the afterlife.

Statues of Anubis often show him with a black jackal head.

Anubis in Art

In artwork, Anubis is often shown as a man with the head of a jackal. Sometimes, he is shown as a black jackal. Ancient Egyptians believed jackals were powerful animals. Jackals were also known for digging up graves. This is why Anubis is connected to them. He is the protector of cemeteries.

The Temple of Seti I contains many carvings of Egyptian gods, including Anubis.

Ancient Egyptians painted images of Anubis on tomb walls. They also carved drawings of him into stone walls. Images of him were carved on ancient Egyptians' sarcophagi too.

This carving of Anubis can be found at the Temple of Seti I at Abydos.

These images often showed scenes of Anubis guiding the spirits of the dead.

Anubis was a guide to ancient Egyptians. He guarded all souls. The role he played in ancient Egyptians' lives and deaths is why he remains one of their most well-known gods.

Dr. Wafaa el-Saddik, former director of the Egyptian Museum in Cairo, Egypt, wrote about Anubis:

> The jackal is most commonly associated with Anubis. . . . He is depicted as a jackal or as a jackal-headed human and is often lying down or sitting on a coffin.

Source: Dr. Wafaa el-Saddik. "Anubis, Upwawet, and Other Deities: Personal Worship and Official Religion in Ancient Egypt." *Egyptian Museum Cairo*, May 1, 2008. 5.

What's the Big Idea?

Read this quote carefully. What is its main idea? Explain how the main idea is supported by details.

LEGENDARY FACTS

Ancient Egyptians believed Anubis guided them through the afterlife.

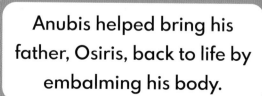

Anubis helped bring his father, Osiris, back to life by embalming his body.

Anubis was known as the jackal-headed god.

The ancient *Book of the Dead* describes how Anubis led a dead person's spirit.

Glossary

afterlife
in ancient Egypt, a place where a person's spirit goes after death

embalming
the process of preserving a dead body

fertility
the ability to produce farm crops or other plant life

rites
religious ceremonies or acts

sarcophagi
stone coffins

shrines
holy places where people or gods are honored

Online Resources

To learn more about Anubis, visit our free resource websites below.

Visit **abdocorelibrary.com** or scan this QR code for free Common Core resources for teachers and students, including vetted activities, multimedia, and booklinks, for deeper subject comprehension.

Visit **abdobooklinks.com** or scan this QR code for free additional online weblinks for further learning. These links are routinely monitored and updated to provide the most current information available.

Learn More

Bell, Samantha S. *Osiris*. Abdo, 2023.

Flynn, Sarah Wassner. *Ancient Egypt*. National Geographic, 2019.

Index

About the Author

Allan Morey grew up on a farm in central Wisconsin. That is where he developed his love for animals and the outdoors. Morey received a Master of Fine Arts degree from Minnesota State University, Mankato, and he has written dozens of books for children. He now lives in Saint Paul, Minnesota, with his wife and their many furry family members.